Fabulous
# Las Vegas

*Front cover: The Strip at night from The Palms*

Published by
Beautiful America Publishing Company
P.O. Box 244
Woodburn, OR 97071

Library of Congress Catalog Number
2006005311

ISBN 0-89802-815-9
ISBN 0-89802-814-0 (paperback)

Copyright © 2006 by Beautiful America Publishing Company

All Rights Reserved
No portion of this book is to be reproduced
in any form, including electronic media
without written permission from the publisher.

Printed in Korea

*Welcome to Fabulous Las Vegas*

FABULOUS
# LAS VEGAS

Photography by Larry Hanna

Text by Jackie Brett

Beautiful America Publishing Company

# Contents

Introduction . . . . . . . . . . . . . . . . . . . . . . . . . . . . . . . . . . . . . . . . 5

Las Vegas / Serious Side of the City . . . . . . . . . . . . . . . . . . . 8

Gaming . . . . . . . . . . . . . . . . . . . . . . . . . . . . . . . . . . . . . . . . . 9

Eras and Trends . . . . . . . . . . . . . . . . . . . . . . . . . . . . . . . . . 12

Hotel-Casinos . . . . . . . . . . . . . . . . . . . . . . . . . . . . . . . . . . . 13

Entertainment . . . . . . . . . . . . . . . . . . . . . . . . . . . . . . . . . . 16

Shopping . . . . . . . . . . . . . . . . . . . . . . . . . . . . . . . . . . . . . . 18

Dining . . . . . . . . . . . . . . . . . . . . . . . . . . . . . . . . . . . . . . . . 22

Weddings . . . . . . . . . . . . . . . . . . . . . . . . . . . . . . . . . . . . . . 23

Resort Attractions . . . . . . . . . . . . . . . . . . . . . . . . . . . . . . . 26

Museums . . . . . . . . . . . . . . . . . . . . . . . . . . . . . . . . . . . . . . 27

Test Site / Art . . . . . . . . . . . . . . . . . . . . . . . . . . . . . . . . . . . 31

Factory Tours . . . . . . . . . . . . . . . . . . . . . . . . . . . . . . . . . . . 36

Vehicle Fascination / Thrill-Seeking Opportunities . . . . 37

Transportation . . . . . . . . . . . . . . . . . . . . . . . . . . . . . . . . . . 40

Fremont Street / The Valley . . . . . . . . . . . . . . . . . . . . . . . 41

Boulder City . . . . . . . . . . . . . . . . . . . . . . . . . . . . . . . . . . . . 48

History . . . . . . . . . . . . . . . . . . . . . . . . . . . . . . . . . . . . . . . . 66

Hoover Dam and Lake Mead / Beyond the Neon . . . . . . 67

Nearby Cities and Towns . . . . . . . . . . . . . . . . . . . . . . . . . 70

The LVCVA and News Bureau . . . . . . . . . . . . . . . . . . . . . 75

About the Author . . . . . . . . . . . . . . . . . . . . . . . . . . . . . . . 78

About the Photographer . . . . . . . . . . . . . . . . . . . . . . . . . 79

# Introduction

Let's get something straight, Las Vegas is not your typical city and that's probably why I love it so much. It is a one-of-a-kind metropolis that thrives on superlatives — biggest, brightest, longest, tallest – and is dedicated to providing fun for everyone. It's a 24/7 town on steroids.

I first encountered Las Vegas as a youngster in 1958 on a trip with my mother. There were only 12 low-rise hotels back then on what is now a three-mile long Strip and naturally being from Chicago we had to stay at the Stardust. After all, we had connections. Back then, everyone had connections even if they didn't know it. It was still Las Vegas' heyday where almost everything was "comped" and the Mob ruled.

The things I remember most were the incredulous summer heat around 115 degrees, the sexy ladies wearing bikinis and high heels, and the headlining shows – we saw Red Skelton at the Sands and The McGuire Sisters at the Desert Inn. We left after a couple days and in my youth, I knew emphatically that I would NEVER live in the decadent city of lights.

Cut to February 1976 when I moved to Las Vegas after living in Hollywood for six years. It wasn't love at first sight. In fact, I looked at the dissolute desert community as a giant kitty-litter box. But gradually things changed. The weather in spite of the intense summer heat, the vast open sky with colorful sunrises and sunsets, and the city's all day - all night voracious thirst for excitement won me over. After nearly 30 years, this is unequivocally home.

*The view of the strip from the Eiffel Tower*

Opposite: Thrill of a Vegas Show

# LAS VEGAS

Las Vegas is the largest city founded in the 20th Century. Being a city that constantly reinvents itself, it is also one of the most changed cities. Just think, the 1,000-room Stardust was huge back then. Who would have ever dreamt that Las Vegas would become the city of mega-resorts? Unless a hotel has 2,000 or more rooms, it's considered small. On just one corner of the Las Vegas Strip at Tropicana Avenue, four hotels: MGM Grand, Tropicana, Excalibur and New York-New York combined have more than 12,000 rooms.

Now we're entering a new era of mega-mergers. MGM/Mirage has merged with Mandalay Bay and together they control the following Strip properties: Mandalay Bay and THEhotel; Luxor; Excalibur; NewYork-NewYork; MGM Grand; Monte-Carlo; Bellagio; The Mirage; Treasure Island (TI); and Circus Circus. The deal between Harrah's and Caesars allows the company to control in Las Vegas: Harrah's; Flamingo; Caesars Palace; Bally's; Paris; the Rio; Bourbon Street, which is closing; and in the future the Imperial Palace.

More hotel expansions are underway and new resorts like Palazzo being built by the Venetian and the W Hotel are under construction. This year, the most anticipated opening was Steve Wynn's new copper-skinned hotel bearing his name…Wynn Las Vegas.

The Vegas skyline is drastically changing. The low-rise city is now going vertical. Time-share and condominium towers are going up all over the valley. This trend began a few years ago when Turnberry and Park Towers at Hughes Center built their luxury high-rise living towers and almost instantly sold out. There's simply no end in sight to this skyward movement.

Phenomenal growth momentum has been synonymous with Las Vegas' destiny. At the turn of the 20th century, it was one of the smallest towns in Nevada and by 1915, the population was a mere 1,500 people.

The population explosion took off big time in the 1980s and for the past 20 or more years, over 6,000 people have been moving into town monthly. Now there are more than a million and a half residents and it's predicted that Nevada will be the fastest growing state for the next 25 years.

The population explosion has been so great that Nevada gained another seat in the U.S. Assembly after the census.

## SERIOUS SIDE OF THE CITY

Tourism is the main industry, so in that sense the major business corridors are the Las Vegas Strip and Fremont Street. Other businesses do exist and the Nevada Development Authority (NDA) and Nevada Economic Development Authority are challenged to convince companies to move here. One of the selling points used to be the low cost of living but that unfortunately is drastically changing. Another drawback is the lack of cultural diversity and educational opportunities. The biggest work forces are in the hotel service and construction industries.

Family life is very different in a 24/7 community. Parents work different shifts and most of the schools are year-round. Typical family life can be rare. The one question visitors always asked was, "Do people really live here?" Most residents would have fun giving answers like, "No, we commute from L.A." or "No, I live in a hotel."

With growth comes challenge. As the nation's fifth largest school district, it has been an impossible task to keep up with the explosion of youth in the valley and build the desperately needed schools. Finding teachers is an equally daunting task.

People have chosen to move to Las Vegas from all over the world. It is a true melting pot mirroring a reflection of what the world is all about…people. To see the humanity mix, look at the dealers and service people.

One thing that is lacking is public parks; however, the newer planned communities like Summerlin and Green Valley have incorporated public grounds.

Growth is the city's biggest challenge. A task force was even put together to consider natural resources, urban planning (now they're thinking about it) and government coordination.

# Gaming

What's interesting about the state of Nevada is more than 100 years ago people migrated to the Silver State to find gold and get rich. Nothing has changed; people still come to Nevada and Las Vegas to get rich. Only now they try to hit on the Mega-bucks machines and win at table games.

From the 1930s until the mid-1970s, table games including blackjack, baccarat and roulette were the mainstay and the dealers were male. It wasn't until slot machines became electronic and video poker machines captured Middle America's hearts that slot machines became the casinos' breadwinners. Casino management was happy because slot machines were less labor intensive.

In the mid-1970s, casinos tried a daring venture having dollar slot banks circling a raised platform with one attendant giving customer service. In order to place a maximum bet, people had to play three to five dollar coins in one machine at a time. Everyone thought people would resist; they would never go for this craziness. Little could anyone predict that within 10 years, there would be slot machines that accepted $500 and $1,000 coins as one bet. What a concept!

Coins dropping into metal bins at the bottom of slot machines used to create the sounds of excitement in a casino. Today everything has changed again and casinos have been switching to the new ticket in-ticket out paper system. They just present their paper ticket that registered the winning amount.

In the 1980s, tournaments entered the gaming scene. Today slot, blackjack, roulette and poker tournaments are a way of life. Poker rooms, thanks to television celebrity tournaments, are growing at a frenetic pace.

Race books started showing up in the late 1930s when they were added as an adjunct to the casino. They evolved into huge Race and Sports Books in many major properties like Caesars Palace, the Las Vegas Hilton and the Stardust, where the trend started with jumbo viewing screens and special privileges. Super Bowl, the Kentucky Derby and major fights always pack these betting areas.

One thing that hasn't changed is casinos trying to attract high-roller players especially the richest of them who are referred to as "whales." Depending on the property, a high roller may even be a middle-income person, but the bottom

*The Sports Book arena at the Las Vegas Hilton*

*Slot players*

*A friendly game of blackjack*

line is they put up a line of credit and they are players.

Years ago, junkets were a way of doing business. Casinos had offices in various strategic cities that lined up big players and flew them on private charters to Las Vegas. As the airlines and casinos changed, junkets became a thing of the past.

Casino security that overlooks the table games and slots encountered a major change. Until the 1980s, there was a surveillance system called the Eye in the Sky. It was a catwalk in the ceiling above the table games that had one-way glass mirrors for management to look through and detect cheating. When security camera systems were invented, the whole surveillance scene changed. Cameras and computers are a much better detection than the human eye, plus they can replay the action. Cameras nowadays make it very difficult to cheat.

Probably the biggest change is casinos used to dictate everything that happened at their property because that was where the money was made. In the early 1980s, the Internal Revenue Service overhauled the city and required every resort department and tip earners to be accountable, which put a real damper on comps. Now the casino is only an income-earning component of the resort's total revenue especially with entertainment, dining and shopping making a big chunk of revenue.

# Eras and Trends

In the past 60 years, Las Vegas had some very distinctive eras defining its existence. The Mob's heyday was in the 1940s especially when Bugsy Siegel built the Flamingo in 1946, but the influence prevailed into the 1970s. Decadence was a way of life.

When Howard Hughes moved into the old Desert Inn, he began gobbling up properties and at one time owned the Silver Slipper, the Desert Inn, the Castaways (where The Mirage now sits), the Sands, the Frontier and the Landmark, which looked like a space needle and was across from the Convention Center.

Billionaire Kirk Kerkorian changed the city three times by building the world's largest hotel with the 5,005-room MGM Grand holding the title for now.

The next move was when corporations bought the resorts and went on the public stock exchange. Suddenly Las Vegas was legit, but with this caveat came the accountants and the declaration that every department had to be accountable. No longer could you give away food, shows and rooms indiscriminately.

Steve Wynn began downtown with his first resort the Golden Nugget and moved onto the Strip in a big way with three elaborate hotels sharing a common element…water. The tropical Mirage has the volcano, Treasure Island the sea battle and Bellagio, the dancing water fountains.

A return to the Sin City quickly began to emerge in the new century and it is hotter than ever with nearly every major hotel having one or more nightclubs. The three-story Studio 54 at the

MGM opened and started the nightclub trend. Now the lounges are so sleek and chic that they are referred to as Ultra Lounges.

The Las Vegas Convention and Visitors Authority's advertising slogan, "What Happens In Vegas, Stays In Vegas" has taken the world by storm and a Sin City Chamber of Commerce plus very decadent and risqué billboards seal the adult image.

The current overwhelming trend is the "Manhattanization" of Las Vegas with it going from a low-rise city to one of high-rises. The movement began with the hotels, but it's being accelerated with condominium towers going up everywhere in the valley. Even Donald Trump is building his tower across from the Fashion Show Mall and Wynn's new resort. About 100 high-rise projects are on the books and if half get built, the look of the city will definitely be forever changed.

## Hotel-Casinos

This is a funny thought, imagine thousands of years from now, an archaeological dig is done in Las Vegas. Do you think they'll be miffed by finding Rome, Egypt, Paris, New York and Venice all in one excavation?

Hotel/casinos used to be notorious for applying tricks of the trade. For starters there were no hotel lobbies. You would find a check-in counter located adjacent to the casino so you would get hooked to gaming from the onset. Today there are actual definable hotel lobbies and some even make grandiose statements like the one at Bellagio with the giant Dale Chihuly chandelier or the opulent lobby at the Venetian with high Italian Renaissance-style painted ceilings, grand arches, marble columns and gold trim.

Now with gaming including Indian casinos in so many places, Las Vegas has succumbed to being a tourist town that competes globally. The new objective is to be the best.

Service is of the utmost importance and quite a challenge considering the thousands of rooms at resorts like the MGM Grand, which with 5,000 rooms holds the current title of the world's largest hotel.

Room amenities are now important and offer a competitive edge. Many rooms are larger, offer technology attributes such as plasma screen televisions and Internet access, provide safes, and give 24-hour room service.

Themed hotels were first introduced in 1966 when Caesars Palace courted the Roman theme and Circus Circus followed in 1968 with the tent-shaped building embellishing the midway treatise with live circus acts performing above the casino. Other themed properties followed like the medieval castle-shaped Excalibur in 1990 and the Egyptian Luxor glass pyramid in 1993. Taking themes one step further, hotels began copying cities…New York-New York, Paris and Venice.

There are many ways resorts make themselves different. One way has been with pools. The Tropicana in 1986 elevated backyard elegance by introducing "The Island of Las Vegas" with three swimming pools, a waterfall, a lagoon and even a couple of swim-up blackjack tables.

A few years later, the Flamingo went further and made a more spectacular 15-acre tropical paradise and added a Wildlife Habitat with animals such as ducks, swans, flamingos, penguins, peacocks and other exotic birds that you can view for free. Mandalay Bay raised the bar with its lush

*The brand new Wynn Hotel and Casino*

*Opposite: The beautiful Bellagio*

11-acre beach environment with foliage, three pools, a lazy river, a topless pool and a magnificent 1.6-million-gallon wave pool with a sand-and-surf beach where major outdoor concerts are also held.

Another significant turning point was when Alexis Park opened in 1984. It was the first successful non-gaming resort. Naysayers said it would never make it. That is truly a joke now as every major non-gaming resort chain imaginable has invaded the valley's marketplace.

## Entertainment

Las Vegas has many titles but "The Entertainment Capital of the World" is practically a trademark. Since the first big-name performer, the Pistol Packin' Mama, Sophie Tucker headlined a two-week engagement in 1944 at the Last Frontier, hotels a few miles from downtown along Highway 91 (now The Strip) began building showrooms and name entertainment on marquees became the norm.

The Rat Pack era made the fifties and sixties memorable. The charisma between Frank Sinatra, Dean Martin, Sammy Davis, Jr. and Joey Bishop was extraordinary. Headliners also visited lounges like the famous one at the Sahara where Louis Prima and Keely Smith with saxophonist Sam Butera and his Witnesses became a major attraction in 1956. Later Don Rickles would make a name for himself in this same lounge by insulting the celebrity hierarchy.

From the '50s through the '70s, two shows were produced nightly starting with dinner and an 8 p.m. performance followed by a midnight cocktail show. Headliners would work one or two-week gigs and do 12 to 14 shows a week. One name that's synonymous with Las Vegas is Wayne Newton, who became the Midnight Idol. He's also known as "Mr. Las Vegas."

The next big transition was production shows with the iconic Las Vegas showgirl, whose height ranges from 5'8" to 6'2". The two remnants of this period that was a staple in the '60s and '70s are the Tropicana's Parisian-themed "Folies Bergere" and "Jubilee!" at Bally's with gigantic special effects like the Sinking of the Titanic. When showgirls went topless, it was both scandalous and a "must-see" attraction at the same time.

The celebrity-impersonator craze began in 1983 with "Legends in Concert" at the Imperial Palace and now there are at least a half-dozen impersonator shows at any given time with Elvis duplicates being the most common.

In the early '80s another quagmire occurred when corporations and the bean counters (accountants) wanted every department to be a profit center. That's when showrooms did away with dinner shows, slowly eliminated cocktail service, cut back on live music, and removed table and booth seating in favor of theater-type seating.

Meanwhile two other types of shows integrated themselves onto the entertainment quilt. Thanks to illusionists Siegfried & Roy and master magician Lance Burton at the Monte Carlo, who each began as variety acts in production spectaculars, magic shows blanket the Strip.

The other mega-change was Steve Wynn's introduction of Cirque du Soleil shows. It took awhile for people to get comfortable with the non-traditional circus shows without

*The "King" in concert at the Imperial Palace*

animals, but today all the biggest resorts have a Cirque extravaganza.

Broadway fare has never prevailed; however, "Mamma Mia" at Mandalay Bay has been the exception. Making the attempt again, Wynn has signed an exclusive with "Avenue Q" and booked "Spamalot," and the Venetian plans to open "Phantom of the Opera." Part of the challenge for Broadway musicals may be the 90-minute show formula created by the Las Vegas visitor's short attention span and the casino's allure.

Headliners are still a mainstay with older acts migrating to off-Strip resorts and major superstars like Celine Dion, Barry Manilow and Elton John trying to get away from touring by settling down in a showroom. Rather intriguing is how some headlining acts such as Clint Holmes at Harrah's, Danny Gans at The Mirage and The Scintas at the Rio are basic unknowns outside of Las Vegas, but prominent stars in town.

Of all the changes, probably the biggest has been the showrooms being turned over to four-wall and two-wall rental deals that have altered the entire way the shows are run in Las Vegas. These deals dictate who is headlining, how tickets are sold, create competition through middle vendors, and cause increased ticket prices.

Along the way, huge arenas like the 12,000-seat Mandalay Bay Events Center, the Orleans Arena, 17,000-seat MGM Grand Arena, 20,000-seat Thomas & Mack Center, and 40,000-seat Sam Boyd Stadium were built making way for touring groups, superstars and mega-events that can and do attract thousands of fans.

Today, Las Vegas is simply an entertainment kaleidoscope.

# SHOPPING

### Fashion Show Mall

There was a time when Las Vegas was a shopping wasteland. The first mall on the Strip was the Fashion Show and it was exceedingly commonplace when it opened in 1977. It has since undergone major overalls and expansions and now has the distinctive Cloud as its signature piece.

The Fashion Show's new Great Hall features an elevated stage and fashion show runway for multi-media presentations of fashion and lifestyle events. The east expansion also has an 11,288-square-foot Food Court with seating for 1,000, a premier Concierge Center offering complete visitor services, and gourmet restaurants overlooking the Strip.

### Forum Shops

Las Vegas went on the world's shopping mall map and told retail attractions like Rodeo Drive and Madison Avenue to move over when Caesars Palace built the phenomenal Forum Shops that has undergone two expansion projects. The mall with 160 shops makes more money per square foot than any mall in the country and gives new meaning to Shopping Kingdom.

When the mall opened, it unveiled a visually stunning, atmosphere-simulating, ancient Roman streetscape with a ceiling emulating a Mediterranean sky going from dark to light. Another attraction is the Atlantis Aquarium with over 500 tropical fish.

The Forum Shops latest Phase III expansion opened on Oct. 22, 2004. Luxurious in every detail, Phase III is a three-level fashion and dining marvel with its sweeping plaza, complete with replicas of the Trevi and Triton Fountains, a glorious massive reflecting pool, dazzling skylight and majestic spiral escalator, the first in the United States until Wynn Las Vegas opened.

### *Canal Shoppes*

The next retail mall deserving of notoriety is The Grand Canal Shoppes at the Venetian. This 500,000-square-foot Venice-themed mall with about 70 retailers winds around a reproduction of Venice's Grand Canal where gondola rides with singing gondoliers are a big attraction. The area also features cobbled walkways and a replica of St. Mark's Square with strolling entertainers.

### *Desert Passage*

Keeping with a theme, the 450,000-square-foot Desert Passage mall at the Aladdin is circular with 140 stores. The décor is reminiscent of the bustling marketplaces of Morocco, Africa and India with an Arabian street theme, a sky effect, lots of live entertainment and a rainstorm show at Merchants' Harbor.

### *Outlet Malls*

For the longest time there were no outlet malls and now there are two huge ones in addition to the Fashion Outlet of Las Vegas mall at Primm. The indoor Las Vegas Outlet Center on Las Vegas Blvd. has 130 outlets, two food courts and a merry-go-round, and the outdoor Las Vegas Premium Outlets downtown has 120 outlets and a food court.

### *Hotel Shopping*

Most of the big hotels like Bellagio, Wynn, Caesars Palace, Bally's, Paris, Rio, and the MGM Grand offer exclusive shopping areas. The biggest is Mandalay Place with a 100,000-square-foot shopping center located on a sky bridge between Mandalay Bay and Luxor resorts.

### *District at Green Valley Ranch*

Just minutes from the airport is The District at Green Valley Ranch, located in Henderson. The District has been billed as a metropolitan "lifestyle" center, comprised of an interesting mix of retail shops, restaurants, office space and luxury lofts above the stores. The heart of The District is its tree-lined "Main Street," flanked by more than 40 specialty retail stores and restaurants. Pedestrians can stroll along cobblestone sidewalks, relax on park benches or even bring Fido to one of the pet-friendly areas.

### *Logo Shops*

Logo shops have been immensely popular since the 1980s when every hotel, attraction, show, themed restaurant and headliner found this lucrative gold mine and great way of advertising. Almost every property, big or small, has a signature shop or retail area.

*The Forum Shops at Caesars*

*Grand Canal Shops at the Venetian*

# Dining

Most large resorts have anywhere from four to a dozen restaurants in order to appeal to a multitude of taste buds and also to hold the interest of the folks staying at the hotel for a few nights. In the past, there was usually a 24-hour coffee shop, a buffet, gourmet room and maybe a casual Mexican or Asian eatery. Now there's an endless array of gourmet options. According to the Nevada Restaurant Association, there are more then 3,200 restaurants.

### *Themed Restaurants*

Las Vegas has its fair share of famous themed restaurants. Most have been successful, usually because of the themed décor rather than the food and once again for selling logo items. Some are free standing and others are inside resorts.

The stand-alone eateries were started when the rock music themed Hard Rock Café was built with the eye-catching giant neon guitar pylon sign. Inside there's music memorabilia all over the walls.

The Harley Davidson Café built on the Strip has made its architectural signature piece a 28-foot-high Harley-Davidson Heritage Softial Classic motorcycle jutting from the building. This place is home to memorabilia documenting 100 years of Harley-Davidson history.

The giant Hofbräuhaus on Paradise Road is an authentic replica of the Munich Hofbräuhaus that was originally commissioned in 1589 by King William V. and it provides an authentic piece of Bavarian culture.

At the Forum Shops, there's the two-story movie-themed Planet Hollywood and inside hotels you'll find NASCAR Café at the Sahara, Rainforest Café at the MGM Grand, ESPN Zone at New York-New York and the Star-Trek themed Quark's Bar and Restaurant at the Las Vegas Hilton. So far the most successful of them all is Jimmy Buffett's festive nautical-themed Margaritaville at the Flamingo. The centerpiece three-story Volcano Bar erupts over the bar, spilling margarita mix into two giant 300-gallon blenders every hour.

The two newest places are Toby Keith's restaurant and bar at Harrah's that has a guitar-shaped bar and the legendary Hollywood rock-'n'-roll music haven Rainbow Bar & Grill across the street from the 'Hard Rock'.

### *Buffets*

We don't need to dwell on buffets, but let it suffice to say there are around 60 buffets and more than 50 have weekend brunches. Today a hotel not having a buffet would be an oddity. Over the years, the biggest changes have been the size of the buffets, as many are enormous, including such things as themed foods, plus carving areas and live actions stations.

### *Gourmet Dining*

Over the past 13 years, the biggest change has been in the gourmet-dining arena. Since the start of Las Vegas' heyday, the resorts always incorporate a high-end restaurant; one that could be used for comping high rollers. While there were excellent restaurants, they weren't associated with world-class chefs. Culinary gurus weren't paying attention to Las

Vegas until 1992 when Wolfgang Puck opened his first Las Vegas eatery, Spago in the Forum Shops at Caesars, and became the first true "celebrity" chef to create a contemporary fine-dining restaurant in the city.

Now Las Vegas can probably lay claim to being the "Dining Capitol of the World" since nearly every major chef in the world is opening an award-winning dining establishment in town. The elite dining movement has been like an avalanche, snowballing into a highly competitive game. Example: The Mandalay Bay has recognized the huge demand for vegetarian food, by installing Chef Hubert Keller in their Fleur de Lys restaurant, and you need reservations to partake of his outstanding full-course gourmet vegetarian delights. The competition has also created some extraordinary dining environments such as Red Square, with more than 170 varieties of chilled vodkas. At Mandalay Bay is Aureole's mind-boggling, 42-foot-high vertical wine tower, built of steel and laminated glass that holds nearly 1,000 bottles.

A whole book can just be written on the high-end restaurants. Over the years, the area off the Strip on Flamingo and Paradise roads has turned into what locals call "Restaurant Row." In just a two-block radius you'll find: Lawry's the Prime Rib, Piero's, McCormick & Schmick's, Cozymel's, Bahama Breeze, Gordon Biersch, Del Frisco's, Firefly, Ruth Chris, Yolie's Brazilian Steakhouse, Marrakech, Morton's, Roy's from Hawaii, Buca Di Beppo and PF Chang's to name only a few.

Visiting Las Vegas with dieting on your mind is very foolhardy. Think like royalty and indulge!

# WEDDINGS

Can we unveil Las Vegas and not talk about it being the matrimonial capitol? Pretty ironic when you figure it became notorious as a place to get a quickie divorce back in the '30s and '40s when there was a guest ranch at the place now known as Floyd Lamb State Park where you could stay while you waited for the divorce paperwork to be completed.

Today, Las Vegas issues more than 100,000 marriage licenses a year and has more than 60 chapels to assist with the vows — the most historic being the freestanding landmark Little Chapel of the West. It was known as the "wedding place of the stars," beginning with Betty Grable and Harry James in 1942, and continuing with many more including Judy Garland to her fourth husband, Mark Herron, on Nov. 13, 1965, and Billy Bob Thornton to Angelina Jolie on May 5, 2000.

In true over-the-top fashion, the Little White Wedding Chapel opened a 24-hour drive-thru window in 1991, after the owner noticed a handicapped couple having difficulty getting out of the car and into the chapel. The chapel is also famous for marrying many stars including Joan Collins, Michael Jordan, Demi Moore and Bruce Willis, Mickey Rooney, Patty Duke, Frank Sinatra and Britney Spears when she did her quickie one-night madcap "I do." This chapel is constantly featured on national television shows.

Since same-day marriages are easy, many famous people have tied the knot and helped put Las Vegas on the matrimonial chart. The list is endless but here's a few noteworthy ones: El Rancho Vegas, Joanne Woodward and Paul Newman in 1958

*The District at Green Valley Ranch*

*Alize dining room at the Palms*

*Las Vegas Hilton Steak House*

and TV sleuth David Janssen the same year; Joan Crawford in 1955 at the Flamingo; Kirk Douglas in 1954 at the Sahara; Bing Crosby and Kathryn Grant in 1957; Elizabeth Taylor and Eddie Fisher in 1959; Mary Tyler Moore and NBC vice-president Grant Tinker in 1962; Frank Sinatra and Mia Farrow at the Sands in 1966; and the most famous "I do" of all – Elvis, 32 to Priscilla Beaulieu, 21 on May 1, 1967 at the Aladdin.

In the late '70s, resorts started putting in their own wedding chapels when they learned it was a lucrative business and today more than 20 resorts have one. Another popular promotion is Web casting your wedding for your long-distance family members and friends. The two biggest marriage days are naturally Valentine's Day, which has had more than 4,000 weddings, and New Year's Eve. But remember one thing; getting married in Las Vegas doesn't secure living happily ever after.

# Resort Attractions

Originally gaming and entertainment were enough of an attraction, but now there's hardly any large resort that doesn't have one or more such magnets. Some attractions are free and others have admission fees. There's really something to suit everyone's interest and budget.

Let's take a whirlwind tour of the incredible free things to see. In front of the hotels, Caesars Palace led the way with its reflection pool in 1966 but Steve Wynn took things to elevated heights when he built the Mirage Volcano that erupts every 15 minutes at night spewing smoke and fire 100 feet in the air. When this visual magnet was introduced, it caused Strip traffic to come to a complete halt.

Wynn went ahead and one upped himself two more times with alluring attractions in front of Treasure Island in 1993, when he started the Buccaneer Bay Sea Battle, the first front yard mega-attraction with live actors. This show had a pyrotechnic battle between a British frigate and a pirate ship, ending with one ship sinking and men jumping overboard into the water for dear life. The show was completely revamped in 2004 and turned into the Sirens of TI to embellish Vegas' current "sex sells" theme. Now temptresses of the sea sing and dance while squaring off with feisty pirates about four times a night.

The Bellagio was next in 1998 with its traffic-stopping, multi-sensory water show. More than 1,000 fountains soar as high as 240 feet into the air and stretch across more than 1,000 feet of the Bellagio Lake. Choreographed to music, it can be heard all over.

Most resorts are more interested in getting people to visit an indoor attraction increasing the odds that visitors may stop and play along the way. There's really no end to the fabulous things you can see.

The Mirage introduced the Royal White Tiger Habitat, the first zoo-like and very high-end animal environment inside a resort featuring tigers. Another aquatic marvel is the massive floor-to-ceiling aquarium that acts as a backdrop to the Mirage's front desk. With the Mirage having tigers, the MGM Grand opened a multilevel Lion Habitat with 35-foot glass walls. Get it…the MGM lion.

Other properties like Circus Circus with its circus acts have opted for free aerial shows. The Tropicana has Air Play featuring live specialty acts performing above the main casino tables. The Rio is the most extravagant with its Masquerade Show in the Sky featuring five ceiling-suspended floats that move and carry entertainers and some visitors along a track to different themed parades.

Another absolutely magnificent free 24-hour offering is the Bellagio Conservatory. Here the flowers and vegetables are changed seasonally to build new compelling themes, whether it is a celebration of spring or a holiday such as Christmas or Chinese New Year. This can be a must-see stop each time someone visits.

Two off-Strip marvels include the 117,000-gallon saltwater aquarium with tropical fish and live hourly mermaid evening shows in the Mermaid at the Silverton lounge. The indoor Mystic Falls Park at Sam's Town on Boulder Highway offers "Sunset Stampede," a dancing water, laser and light show.

Many indoor resort attractions require an admission fee but again offer a multitude of special-interest possibilities.

The Las Vegas Hilton appeals to trekkies with Star Trek: The Experience. Here visitors can move into the 24th century with two featured motion-sensory rides.

If it's celebrities that peak your curiosity, then Madame Tussauds Interactive Wax Attraction at the Venetian is where you can hug and touch more than 100 of them and snap your own photos.

For people who like a view, there's the 50-story high Eiffel Tower Tour that replicates the experience in France, only at a two-thirds scale.

Mandalay Bay has Shark Reef with 2,000 aquatic animals representing 100 species from the world's tropical waters. The Mirage has Siegfried & Roy's Secret Garden and Dolphin Habitat.

## Museums

As surprising as it may seem, Las Vegas does have a wide variety of museums, but none of them are huge like in some principal cities. Most are great for occupying a few hours of time.

One of the most popular and well attended is the Liberace Museum located a couple miles east of the Strip at 1775 E. Tropicana Avenue. Two separate buildings host exhibits of the late pianist's collections of pianos, cars, sequined costumes, flashy jewelry, memorabilia and gifts from admirers. Liberace's nearby home, now called The Las Vegas Villa, can

*The Canyon Blaster at Circus Circus*

*Opposite: The colorful and exciting Shark Reef at the Mandalay Bay*

be rented for special occasions. The Villa, which was originally two separate homes and spans 20,000 square feet of elegance, was one of seven homes Liberace owned around the West before his death in 1987. His nickname was "Mr. Showman," but if he were alive today, he'd be known as the "King of Bling" because of all his rings and shiny costumes.

The Elvis-A-Rama Museum pays tribute to another Las Vegas celebrity icon. Located behind the Fashion Show Mall at 3401 Industrial Road, this exhibition features more than $6 million of authentic inventory of Elvis' personal items including his blue suede shoes. The memorabilia business is being sold with word that a bigger Elvis tribute attraction will open on the Strip.

While Las Vegas isn't really a family destination, it does have a couple museums that appeal to youth. One is the Marjorie Barrick Museum of Natural History on the University of Nevada – Las Vegas (UNLV) campus. It focuses on archaeology, anthropology and natural history of the Southwest and Central America.

The Las Vegas Natural History Museum located just north of Fremont Street at 900 Las Vegas Blvd. North focuses on Nevada's wildlife and offers an animated dinosaur exhibit, a diorama of Southern Nevada, a shark exhibit featuring a 3,000-gallon aquarium, a children's hands-on room and popular traveling exhibits. This growing museum has a Smithsonian affiliation.

Across the street is the Lied Discovery Children's Museum with over 100 hands-on exhibits in the arts, humanities and sciences plus traveling displays, programs and entertainment.

King Tut's Tomb and Museum located inside the Luxor is the only full-scale authentic reproduction of Howard Carter's famous 1922 discovery of King Tutankhamun's tomb outside of Egypt.

Opened in 2005, The Atomic Testing Museum is the newest treasure keeper located at 755 E. Flamingo Road. It explores the role the Nevada Test Site played in the Cold War by using photographs of the '50s, which provides a chance to see artifacts and access to the federal Nuclear Testing Archive, and an opportunity to enter the Ground Zero Theater to experience what the Test Site was like during its heyday with atomic testing.

The Nevada Test Site is also where Area 51 exists; however, the government to this day insists there is no such place. Oh, please! Behind this area that supposedly doesn't exist is a tiny village called Rachel located on the world's only Extraterrestrial Highway that is known globally for its alien sightings and making visitors think they're in "The Twilight Zone."

## Test Site

It might be 65 miles outside Las Vegas, but in 1951, the Nevada Test Site was the Silver State's best-known feature. From 1951 to 1992, nearly 1,000 nuclear blasts occurred at the proving ground. The vast outdoor laboratory and national experimental center is larger than the state of Rhode Island taking up approximately 1,375 square miles. It is one of the largest restricted-access areas in the United States. The remote site is surrounded by thousands of additional acres of land withdrawn from the public domain creating an unpopulated landmass comprising some 5,470 square miles.

The U.S. Department of Energy, National Nuclear Security Administration Nevada Site Office provides free general interest tours on a monthly basis that are very interesting and probably one of the most non-Vegas experiences a person can have. You depart Las Vegas by bus and each tour usually covers about 250 miles. Because the Test Site is restricted, visitors must apply well in advance for security clearance.

## Art

This may sound like an odd comment, but in many respects, there are fine pockets of art all around the valley. Certain samples are encased in small museums like those in some hotels that stay open late at night and other art, particularly statuary, is extremely prevalent throughout places like Caesars Palace, Monte Carlo, the Venetian resorts, and the Forum Shops.

Michelangelo spent more than two years carving his David from stone cut in a quarry near Carrera, Italy. Stone from that same quarry was used to create the exact replica of David at Caesars Palace. The Statue of David in the Appian Way shopping arcade stands more than 18 feet high, weighs more than nine tons, cost $50,000 to produce and $100,000 to ship from Turin, Italy.

Also at Caesars Palace, the sculpted statues at the outside pool include an exact replica of Giovanni Bologna's "Rape of the Sabines."

The artistic detail done on the hotels especially the ones with themes and even many retail businesses often carries through to even the doorknobs you unwittingly grab. Competitive custom-designed doorknobs are often trademarks. Many like the Sahara, Riviera, Fitzgeralds and the opulent Bellagio use the hotel's first letter, others embellish a theme like parrot door handles for the Rio, a bucking bronco for Texas Station, a pyramid for the Luxor, a torch like the Statute of Liberty holds for New York-New York, and an electric guitar for the Hard Rock to name only a few.

*Fiery volcanic eruption at the Mirage*

Probably the most famous outlet for viewing art in Las Vegas is The Guggenheim Hermitage Museum located in the Venetian and managed by the Solomon R. Guggenheim Foundation. The museum was conceived as a venue for the presentation of exhibitions based on the collections of the Guggenheim and Hermitage museums. Exhibitions change approximately twice a year.

Located at the heart of the elegant Bellagio resort is the Bellagio Gallery of Fine Art, which is Las Vegas' premier art gallery. Each year the gallery presents exhibitions of artwork and objects drawn from internationally acclaimed museums and private collections.

Valuable artwork also adorns the walls at the French-Mediterranean award-winning restaurant Picasso at Bellagio. Here while you're dining, you'll find an awesome profusion of original Picasso oils and ceramics.

Steve Wynn, known for his exquisite taste, displays his own personal collection of diverse artwork featuring more than a dozen paintings by artists such as Paul Gauguin, Claude Monet, Pablo Picasso, etc. at The Wynn Collection located in his masterful new resort. Some of his gems are Picasso's "Le Rêve," which is coincidentally the name of his Cirque du Soleil show and was the original name of his resort, Rembrandt's "Self-Portrait," "The Persian Robe" by Henri Matisse, and "Peasant Woman Against a Background of Wheat" by Vincent van Gogh.

The Mandalay Bay House of Blues Restaurant and private Foundation Room both inject the city with truly colorful, vivid and imaginative African-American folk art images from the Mississippi Delta region in the Deep South.

The local Las Vegas Art Museum is located more than 10 miles west of the Strip at 9600 W. Sahara Avenue. This museum located inside of a $20 million library facility emphasizes contemporary art, stressing art after post-modernism and featuring changing exhibits.

A most unusual art-type museum is the outdoor Neon Museum with signs on display along Fremont Street. The museum officially "opened" with the installation of its first refurbished sign, The Hacienda Horse and Rider, on Nov. 15, 1996, at the intersection of Las Vegas Blvd. and Fremont Street. This fabulous sign was installed in 1967 at the original Hacienda Hotel.

Of course, the city's most famous sign is actually a landmark. The Welcome Sign, designed by local artist Betty Willis and created by Western Electric Display in 1959, still sits at its original site at the south end of the Strip and is the backdrop to thousands of photos.

There are so many other unusual places to find masterpieces. A major one is the world-renowned artist Dale Chihuly's chandelier - the Fiori di Como, which is a 40,000-pound glass artwork with 2,000 hand-blown colorful glass flowers hanging over the Bellagio lobby and dramatically adorning the ceiling. It is the artist's largest installation to date.

Another glass wonder is Sunset Station's Gaudi Bar, a marvel of brilliant stained glass, tile, and curvilinear forms reminiscent of Antonio Gaudi's Casa Mila in Barcelona.

There's also quite a profusion of public art in the valley. If you arrive or depart via the D gates at McCarran International

*The lush Sam's Town Atrium*

*Fun at Spacequest*

Airport, you will run into David Phelps' horned lizard sculpture on the floor. Another ground swell is the Serpent Mound by Lloyd Hamrol at the Green Valley Library.

There are also bronze statues scattered about. At the Las Vegas Hilton just outside the Race and Sports Book you can see the famous horse Man O' War with his jockey. Known as "Big Red," the legendary chestnut thoroughbred raced in 1919 and 1920 and won 20 of his 21 races. Man O' War retired to a successful 27-year stud career and sired 64 stakes winners and a Triple Crown Winner, War Admiral. He also sired outstanding fillies that foaled 124 stakes winners.

The Las Vegas Hilton has a life-size bronze statue of Elvis!

Two striking, 30-foot high Winged Figures of the Republic sculptures on top of Hoover Dam contain more than four tons of statuary bronze and may be the largest monumental bronzes ever cast in the United States.

The MGM Lion Statue is the largest bronze statue in the Western Hemisphere. It is 45 feet tall by 50 feet long, weighs 50 tons, and is made up of 1,660 pieces of bronze welded together. The sculptor was Snell Johnson, and the designer was M. Smeaton.

The Green Valley Outdoor Sculpture Museum is one of my subtle favorites. Randomly placed along Green Valley Parkway are six magnificent bronze lifelike statues of everyday people doing routine activities created by artist J. Seward Johnson. Despite the bronze coloring of the faces, their casual poses and meticulously detailed clothing cause viewers to do double takes.

# FACTORY TOURS

The area still provides a couple of factory tours even though three – Cranberry World, Kidd (then Kraft) Marshmallow and Ron Lee's World of Clowns have opened and closed over the past couple decades. The remaining ones are free and at the end of each tour is a conveniently located brand-named gift shop.

The self-guided Ethel M® Chocolate Factory tour is extremely popular along with its adjoining 2.5-acre Botanical Cactus Garden, which is an arid landscape rich with cactus, succulents and desert plants from the Southwest and other deserts of the world. It is Nevada's largest and one of the world's biggest collections of its kind with more than 350 species of plants. Over the Christmas holidays, the Cactus Garden is trimmed with thousands of lights creating a majestic sight to behold.

Off the Strip and I-15 is where you can find the National Vitamin Company manufacturing plant with the only free self-guided daily tours in the United States that show each step of making a vitamin along with a history and informational section. The tour is started with cosmetics skin and hair care production. For the children, there's a chance to meet Dino - The Kids Chewable Vitamin Mascot.

## Vehicle Fascination

A fascination with cars and motorcycles seems to be synonymous with Las Vegas.

In the early days, the Imperial Palace Antique Car Museum was the main focus for car enthusiasts. A few years ago, it became The Auto Collections where not only are there more than 250 special-interest cars on display daily, but they are also for sale.

Taking car sales and lots in a new direction, Steve Wynn opened Nevada's exclusive, factory-authorized Ferrari and Maserati dealership adjacent to the main lobby inside his new hotel. The facility features separate new and pre-owned showrooms, a full-service facility and a retail boutique with upscale Ferrari and Maserati merchandise.

At the Forum Shops is an Exotic Cars at Caesars Palace dealership, which is the largest retailer in the Forum Shops. There are more than 50 rare exotic luxury cars on display in the two-tiered showroom.

Another outlet for viewing fabulous vehicles as works of art is the Carroll Shelby Museum located in North Las Vegas at the entrance to the Las Vegas Motor Speedway. Here you can see some of the creations of this gifted designer/artist, who as an auto industry legend has been inducted into the Automotive Hall of Fame. Hours for touring are limited

The factory-authorized Las Vegas Harley-Davidson/Buell® dealership on Eastern and Sahara avenues is the world's largest Harley-Davidson dealership with plenty of bikes for rent and a huge parking lot where riding lessons are taught.

At the Primm Valley Resort in Primm, Nevada, via an historic display, you can step back in time and visit the era of legendary Bonnie and Clyde as you scan the bullet holes and shattered windows of the couple's car and read of their infamous past during the days of the Depression.

You may know him as "Scarface" or one of the most well-known gangsters of the 20th century, and at the same resort you can see Al Capone's bulletproof car.

## Thrill-Seeking Opportunities

Not wanting to leave any market segment unturned, Las Vegas embraces thrill-seeking adventures. If you want to jump off a building without killing yourself, there's always AJ Hackett Bungee Jumping next to Circus Circus.

A few indoor rock-climbing opportunities exist in the valley. The best, natural outdoor rock climbing is in the Red Rock Canyon National Conservation Area. On the Strip, people are scaling a wall at GameWorks in the Showcase Mall in front of the MGM Grand.

While outdoor skydiving opportunities exist, Flyaway just a block off the Strip offers indoor skydiving in a vertical wind tunnel.

Roller coasters definitely fall into this category and five uniquely different tracks provide exciting ups and downs, twists and turns. Unlike a normal theme park with all the rides together, Las Vegas has them spread out amongst properties.

The need-for-speed solutions can be found at the Las Vegas Motor Speedway complex, the crown jewel of auto racing,

*The wave pool at Mandalay Bay*

*Monorail passes the Las Vegas Hilton*

located about 12 miles north of downtown. This is the home of the annual spring NASCAR race, Nevada's biggest annual sporting event attracting 156,000 fans at the 1.5-mile superspeedway. This venue also features a motorsports gift shop and a variety of events on more than a dozen tracts.

Other potential adventures in the valley include soaring, hot air balloon rides, ATV tours and laser tag. For minor thrills, there are numerous motion simulator rides, roller-skating and ice-skating.

## Transportation

Due to the valley's burgeoning growth, Las Vegas is suffering from gridlock. Plus when you mix people moving in from so many different places, their driving or lack of driving skills vary greatly as do their tempers. The major highway arterials into Las Vegas are I-15 coming in from southern California and Utah, and U.S. 95 and 93 that run north and south through the state. In the past 10 years, more freeway extensions are popping up and making a sort of ring around the valley.

So far, valet parking at the hotels is free except for a tip and there is free self-parking except at the downtown municipal lots and the Showcase Mall in front of the MGM Grand.

McCarran International Airport is now ranked as the sixth busiest airport, whereas there was only one small terminal in 1976. Another terminal is under construction and another airport called Ivanpah is being proposed in the desert between Las Vegas and the California border. To learn about the history of McCarran Airport, you can visit the free Howard W. Cannon Aviation Museum located above the baggage claim area at the airport.

McCarran, operating in the outskirts of town in 1950, served 71,660 passengers. Today the airport boasts over 41,000,000 passengers and is in the very heart of Las Vegas, with a proximity to the Strip that can be envied by most tourism destinations.

In the 1980s, the monorail mode of transportation was introduced by Circus Circus to transport guests from the main building to the second tower and RV Park. Over the years a couple more short hauls were introduced and still exist between Treasure Island - The Mirage – Monte Carlo and the Excalibur – Luxor – Mandalay Bay.

In 1995, the $25 million monorail between the MGM Grand and Bally's opened and was eventually closed in order for it to be absorbed by the newest transportation mode, which is the controversial $79 million Las Vegas Monorail that opened July 16, 2004, after more than a seven-month delay. It runs from the MGM Grand to the Sahara and makes a total of seven stops that include the Las Vegas Hilton, Las Vegas Convention Center, Harrah's / Imperial Palace, Flamingo, and Bally's/Paris. Time will determine its success.

There is now a valley transit bus system that didn't exist for many years except on the Strip, which has always been a popular route to the downtown area.

In the 1990s, the Las Vegas Strip Trolley began. It's a green gasoline-powered bus painted to look a San Francisco trolley that stops at most major Strip hotels and runs daily from Mandalay Bay to the Stratosphere.

Taxis are still a viable way to get around and you'll find them lined up at the airport and hotel entrances. What isn't so easy to catch, is a taxi when you get off the beaten path.

## FREMONT STREET

Many visitors never venture downtown to the Fremont Street Experience, which is really the heart of Las Vegas and where the city began. The street was named after Army Lieutenant John Charles Fremont, whose large expedition party arrived in the desert oasis on May 3, 1844.

During the early days of Prohibition in 1924, the population was just under 2,000 and unpaved Fremont Street inaugurated the Automobile Age. The sleepy little railroad town was drastically changed in 1931; however, when gambling became legal again in the Silver State in March of 1932, Fremont Street began a major face-lift with the opening of Pietro Orlando Silvagni's Apache Hotel on the northwest corner of Fremont and Second streets, which is where Binion's now stands. It was the town's first three-story building, had the town's first elevator, and was Vegas' first 100-room hotel.

By 1950, Fremont Street became Glitter Gulch, a neon-clustered main street with a concentration of gaming clubs and 24-hour action. Fremont Street was dubbed the world's brightest cityscape.

On May 18, 1956, the tallest building in Nevada opened, which was the $6 million, 155-room, 15-story Fremont.

On December 14, 1995, the Fremont Street Experience, the $70-millon, four-block-long, open-mesh concave canopy studded with more than two million programmable bulbs and 500 concert-quality speakers made its debut. Combined, the elements present eight-minute light-and-sound shows on the largest electric sign in the world. Nine years later, the Fremont Street Experience revealed its upgraded technology with 12 million light-emitting diodes.

While at times Fremont Street ends up being the Strip's stepchild, it has its own very special personality. For one thing, all the resorts are close together dotting two sides of the street in a concentrated four-block area. The oldest property is the Golden Gate. Downtown's jewel resort is the Golden Nugget. Fitzgeralds is the first black-owned Vegas casino property. For years, one of the big draws was for visitors to have their free picture taken in front of a $1 million horseshoe-shaped display at Binion's Horseshoe. It is now just Binion's since Harrah's took the Horseshoe name and the famous World Series of Poker challenge.

The other properties downtown include the Fremont, Four Queens, Las Vegas Club and the Plaza. A few properties, Main Street Station, the California, Lady Luck and Gold Spike happily exist a mere block off the beaten path.

A few blocks up Fremont Street is the El Cortez that opened on Oct. 29, 1941. The 1941 wing still stands and it's the oldest original casino building in Las Vegas.

## THE VALLEY

There are many misconceptions about Las Vegas. To set the record straight, the actual city of Las Vegas takes in an elongated east-to-west section of the valley that includes Fremont Street, the downtown area and ends at Sahara

*Old Fremont Street*

*Fremont Street today*

*Fremont Hotel and Casino*

Avenue, where Clark County takes over.

The other communities that make up the valley are North Las Vegas, Summerlin, Henderson and Lake Las Vegas.

### *North Las Vegas and Nellis Air Force Base*

Located at the northern tip of the Las Vegas Valley, North Las Vegas is one of Nevada's fastest growing cities with 147,877 people as of January 2004. North Las Vegas is located in Clark County. Four major resorts, Texas Station, Fiesta Rancho, Santa Fe Station and the Cannery are spread out in this region.

North Las Vegas is also home to Nellis Air Force Base (AFB) located approximately eight miles northeast of downtown Las Vegas. Nellis was named in honor of First Lt. William Harrell Nellis, a local flyer killed in action over Germany during WWII. The base covers more than 11,000 acres, while the total land area occupied by Nellis and its restricted ranges is more than 5,000 square miles. An additional 7,700 square miles of airspace north and east of the restricted ranges is also available for military flight operations. That's why you can often drive out near the base or towards the Nevada Test Site and spot aerial maneuvers over the wide open desert.

Nellis AFB, an integral part of the United States Air Force's Air Combat Command (ACC), is known as the "Home of the Fighter Pilot" because it is the mecca of advanced air combat aviation training. Nellis' work force of approximately 10,000 military and civilian personnel makes it one of the largest single employers in southern Nevada.

The pride of the base is the Air Force's aerobatic flight team, the U.S. Thunderbirds that performed their first show as Nellis Air Force Base residents on June 23, 1956. Group tours of Nellis Air Force Base or the Thunderbird Museum can be arranged.

### *Summerlin*

Summerlin is a master-planned community in Las Vegas that's unfolding along the western rim of the Las Vegas Valley in the shadow of the Spring Mountain Range and Red Rock Canyon National Conservation Area. The community with the splendor of its natural surroundings has ranked as America's best-selling master-planned community 10 out of 11 years.

Two major resorts in this vicinity are the Suncoast and the exclusive JW Marriott golf and spa resort. They will be joined in the future by the Red Rock Resort & Casino.

### *Henderson*

Henderson, originally called Basic Townsite, was actually "born in America's defense" 10 years prior to its incorporation during World War II with the building of the Basic Magnesium Plant. The plant supplied the U.S. War Department with magnesium for munitions and airplane parts, which helped the United States and its allies win the war. The town was renamed Henderson in 1944.

In 1947, magnesium production was no longer necessary for defense and most of the 14,000 Basic Magnesium Plant employees moved away leaving well over half the town site's houses, built to house plant workers, vacant. In 1947, the United States War Asset Administration actually offered

Henderson for sale as war surplus property.

In an effort to save the city, the Nevada Legislature spent a weekend visiting Henderson and evaluating the possibility of state administration of Basic Magnesium. Within days of the visit, the legislators unanimously approved a bill giving the Colorado River Commission of Nevada the authority to purchase the industrial plants. Governor Vail Pittman signed the Bill that saved Henderson from becoming war surplus property.

Henderson, with its population of 7,410, was originally about 13 square miles in size. Today, the City of Henderson has grown to more than 94.5 square miles and is the second largest city in Nevada. The city's official slogan "Henderson— a Place to Call Home" reflects a community that enjoys small-town values while benefiting from big-city efficiencies.

Henderson is nationally recognized for its outstanding parks and recreation system, having obtained national accreditation and receiving recognition for Excellence in Parks and Recreation Administration. It also has an extensive trail system (jogging, biking, etc.).

The city boasts the largest recreational facility – the Multigenerational Facility at Liberty Pointe – in Nevada, as well as Nevada's only scenic Bird Preserve. The city supports a variety of cultural events like the nearly 20-year-old "Shakespeare in the Park" and enjoys art programs and productions at The Pavilion at Liberty Pointe, the largest outdoor amphitheater of its kind in Nevada.

Henderson is located just a few miles from McCarran International Airport, and the Henderson Executive Airport, recently acquired by Clark County, is planned for major renovation and development as a reliever airport to McCarran.

Of all the cities within Clark County, Henderson has perhaps the brightest future for Southern Nevada. Henderson's 25 master-planned communities are looked at as models throughout the southwestern United States. Developers fund roads, water, sewer and other infrastructure through Limited Improvement Districts and also contribute land for schools, parks and fire stations. The costs for this infrastructure and amenities are included in the sale price of the home.

### *Lake Las Vegas*

When I attended the groundbreaking ceremony in the middle of the desert years ago for a project called Lake Las Vegas, my thoughts were surely this development would never come to fruition. In the mid-1980s, Ronald F. Boeddeker, President and Chairman of Transcontinental Properties, Inc. envisioned a body of water surrounded by an unparalleled, Mediterranean resort destination showcasing mountains, homes, golf courses, hotels, gaming, restaurants, and boutiques. That vision is now a reality in spite of the daunting challenge of building a dam in the middle of the desert.

Lake Las Vegas is a recreational amenity to Lake Las Vegas Resort, but it also provides approximately 10,000 acre-feet of water storage for the resort's landscape and golf course irrigation requirements.

The private SouthShore Golf Club opened in 1995, and was the first private Jack Nicklaus Signature Golf Course in Nevada. The first resort residents moved in the following year. With the opening of Reflection Bay Golf Club, a Jack

*The Pavilion at Liberty Pointe, Henderson*

*Lake Las Vegas*

Nicklaus Signature Golf Course, in 1998, and The Falls Golf Club, a Tom Weiskopf Design, in 2002, the Lake Las Vegas Resort has been established as a premier golf destination winning numerous prestigious awards.

To date, Lake Las Vegas Resort encompasses exquisite residential offerings in 19 communities, including custom home sites, waterfront and golf villas, resort condominiums and luxury executive homes. The area's most famous resident is singer Celine Dion. Also within the 3,592-acre master planned community are world-class resorts, including the AAA Five Diamond-rated Ritz-Carlton, the AAA Four Diamond-rated Hyatt Regency, and the MonteLago Village offering water-edge restaurants and quaint boutiques. The next resort to build will be the first Loews Hotel upscale chain resort in Nevada.

## BOULDER CITY

Boulder City is one of Nevada's most charming communities and an unexpected oasis located 27 miles southeast of Las Vegas off US 95 and just a few miles from Hoover Dam. The elevated tranquil city with the largest geographical area in the state remains to this day, the only city in Nevada where gaming is not legal. With a population around 15,000 people, Boulder City residents maintain a quaint, small-town atmosphere with a low crime rate because they've instituted a slow-growth policy.

Boulder City was built by the Six Companies and the U.S. Government and designed as a model city to provide homes for the workers building Hoover Dam. The Federal Government owned the entire town for nearly 30 years until January 1960 when it was turned over to the State of Nevada. Boulder City is still very much a government town, with many of its residents working for the National Park Service, Bureau of Reclamation, Nevada Department of Fish & Game, Department of Energy, Bureau of Land Management, and Western Area Power Administration.

A major focal point in the center of town is the classic Dutch Colonial-style Boulder Dam Hotel that was built in 1933 with 61 rooms, and the first Nevada hotel placed on the National Register of Historic Places in 1982. The hotel was built to accommodate visiting government and corporate project managers supervising the building of Hoover Dam, but it quickly became a classy hideaway for some of Hollywood's biggest stars including John Wayne, Shirley Temple, Ronald Coleman, Bette Davis, James Cagney and Will Rogers. Today the hotel is home to the Boulder City Art Guild and Gallery and the Boulder City Hoover Dam Museum, and offers 22 newly remodeled rooms and suites for rent plus a restaurant.

Boulder City has quite a roster of events including the 4th of July Damboree Parade and Celebration, Chautauqua, and the annual Art in the Park.

*Casino MonteLago, Lake Las Vegas*

*The Flamingo Hotel and Casino*

*Flamingo Pool*

*MGM Grand Lion*

*MGM Grand Hotel and Casino*

*Colorful New York-New York Hotel and Casino*

*Luxor Art*

*The Statue of Liberty at New York-New York*

*Luxor Hotel and Casino*

Excalibur Hotel and Casino

Opposite: Circus Circus at night

*Paris Hotel and Casino*

*Eiffel Tower at the Paris*

*The pool at Caesars Palace*

Caesars Palace

*The Rio Hotel and Casino*

Venetian Hotel and Casino

Towering Stratosphere Hotel and Casino

"Howdy Partner," from Vegas Vic

His sweetheart, Vegas Vicky

*Las Vegas Convention Center*

*Mandalay Convention Center*

*Stunning Las Vegas Showgirl in mirror image*

# History

Human history in Southern Nevada extends back more than 10,000 years to man's arrival in the Southwest. The first people positively identified in this region were known as the Anasazi and Basketmakers. Before the white man arrived in the area in 1826, the first settlers were Puebloans followed by the nomadic Southern Paiute, who occupied a good part of Southern Nevada for 7,000 years. They found animal, water and vegetation resources bountiful.

Their history is best depicted in Overton about an hour's drive northeast of Las Vegas at the Lost City Museum that was established in 1935 by the National Park Service to exhibit artifacts that were being excavated. Here you can even see replicas of adobe pueblo houses and the museum, which was constructed of sun-dried adobe brick in a pueblo-revival style. The museum is currently owned and maintained by the State of Nevada as one of its six state museums and the gift shop sells Indian-made jewelry and pottery.

Mormon missionaries headed by Brigham Young first arrived in the marshy meadows in 1855 on their journey between Utah and Arizona or California. They would stop for water and wanted to establish their church in a place that was teeming with Paiute Indians and drifting traders. The result was the Mormon Fort that they built, which is the valley's oldest structure and now a museum located in front of Cashman Field and next to the Las Vegas Natural History Museum.

Contrary to popular belief, there are some places where you can learn about Southern Nevada's history. Two museums that promote the area's history are the Nevada State Museum in Lorenzi Park and the Clark County Heritage Museum in Henderson off Boulder Highway.

# Hoover Dam and Lake Mead

Water is one of the valley's most precious commodities. Ironically this oasis in the desert was blessed with artesian springs that Spanish explorers found when they passed through the Mojave Desert valley in 1829. In Spanish, Las Vegas means "the meadows."

The Indians and early Mormon settlers survived the harsh desert conditions long before air conditioning because of water. But the mighty Colorado River used to run rampant and it took the building of Hoover Dam to tame it.

On September 30, 1935, Boulder Dam was dedicated by President Franklin D. Roosevelt. It was referred to as Boulder Dam because it was derived from the Boulder Canyon Act of 1928. The dividing landmark between Nevada and Arizona was later renamed Hoover Dam.

The government erected its own town one mile from the dam and called it Boulder City. On April 20, 1931, work officially began on Hoover Dam and contractors were given seven years to complete the engineering marvel. Six Companies, Inc., the primary contractor, finished it in 1936. Hoover Dam provided jobs for a work force of 5,000 during the Great Depression.

After the dam was completed, Lake Mead was created by literally flooding a desert valley. The largest manmade lake in the Western Hemisphere, Lake Mead is located 30 miles from Las Vegas and offers freshwater sports of fishing, boating, water skiing, and sailing, attracting thousands of visitors each year. Lake Mead sits in an area known as the Lake Mead National Recreation Area, which provides miles of desert landscape for hiking or enjoying the Northshore Scenic Drive on highway 167 running from Overton to Boulder City.

# Beyond the Neon

While everyone associates Las Vegas with the neon lights, you can travel less than an hour in many different directions and encounter God's country. For many visitors, day trips are the most memorable.

One tourism selling point has always been that in the winter you could go snow skiing at Lee Canyon an hour away in one direction and on the same day drive 40-mintues from town in the opposite direction and be water skiing on Lake Mead.

There are many gorgeous places to visit. If you take a one-hour drive 45 miles to the northwest, you can take in Mt. Charleston. You'll start a slow descent that will escalate suddenly to an elevation where you'll be surrounded by pines and other trees and view the 12,000-foot-high Mt. Charleston, which is the highest mountain in the Toiyabe National Forest. Outdoor activities include horseback riding, hiking, and camping. Near the top is the Mt. Charleston Lodge where you can dine, take winter sleigh rides or spring hayrides, and enjoy a potent Mt. Charleston Coffee.

If you visit the other side of Mt. Charleston by going close to an hour's drive straight out Charleston Avenue, you will run into the Red Rock Canyon National Recreation Area. Years ago it was free to make the drive around the one-way, 13-mile loop that has viewing stops along the way. Today

*Hoover Dam*

*Lake Mead*

there is a fee but an interpretive visitor's center was built at the entrance to the park and it is free to visit.

This natural wonder has a dramatic red-and-gold desert-sandstone landscape. Natural springs, unusual rock formations, and a variety of canyons make it a perfect landscape for hiking, picnicking, bicycling and rock climbing. In the spring, you'll discover desert wild flowers blooming, and all year long you'll encounter the wild burros, which you are asked not to feed.

A little further up the road you will find the Spring Mountain Ranch located within the Red Rock Canyon National Conservation Area and beneath the colorful cliffs of the magnificent Wilson Range. The many springs in these mountains provided water for Paiute Indians and later brought mountain men and early settlers to the area. This 520-acre oasis was developed into a combination working ranch and luxurious retreat. Visitors can tour the main house and ranch, and during the summer, popular musical plays are staged outdoors under the open sky.

If you take an hour's drive 52 miles northeast on I-15 going towards Utah, you'll discover Valley of Fire, Nevada's first state park. The area got its name from the colorful sandstone formations and the changing effects of sunlight on the red, pink, and orange surfaces that can look like flames. Many of the rock formations in the 26,000-acre park have been named for the things they resemble. There's Beehive Rock, Poodle Rock and the more famous naturally sculpted petrified pachyderm – Elephant Rock.

# Nearby Cities and Towns

You can look at Las Vegas as an island surrounded by expansive barren desert land instead of water. The closest cities and towns Mesquite, Searchlight, Laughlin, Jean, and Primm are all less than two hours away and they make for nice getaways.

### *Mesquite*

Going east you'll find Mesquite, a border town on the Utah state line and one of Nevada's fastest growing areas. In the mid-1800's, the Old Spanish Trail and the Mormon Road passed through Mesquite Flats along the Virgin River. In 1894 six young families from nearby Bunkerville rebuilt the irrigation canal and established themselves permanently and shortened the name to Mesquite.

To learn more, visit the Virgin Valley Heritage Museum. It is dedicated to the preservation of the pioneer heritage, culture and history of Mesquite and the Virgin Valley. Significant changes came to Mesquite in 1984 as the town incorporated and growth brought more resorts including the Casa Blanca Resort, Virgin River Hotel and Casino and eight others. Today Mesquite boasts six "world class" championship golf courses including the highly rated Arnold Palmer-designed Oasis Golf Club.

### *Searchlight*

If you travel south to Laughlin, mid-way on the trip, you will pass through the historic mining town of Searchlight that sits just 14 miles up the hill from beautiful Cottonwood Cove on Lake Mohave. The Cottonwood Cove Resort and Marina is located inside Lake Mead National Recreation Area and administered by the National Park Service.

As a living ghost town and the place where U.S. Senator Harry Reid was raised, initial discoveries of predominately gold ore were first made in 1897. The town's boom began in 1902 and peaked in 1907. During this time, the mining town's population of 1,500 was more than Las Vegas, but by 1927, only 50 people were left in Searchlight that at one time had 300 mining claims.

### Laughlin

In a few short decades, the sliver of a town nestled along the Colorado River dividing it from Bullhead, Arizona, is the fast-growing tourist gambling destination known as Laughlin. Many people when they visit feel like they are stepping back in time to when Las Vegas was a young town, only the resorts are larger.

In 1964, Don Laughlin, owner of Las Vegas' 101 Club, flew over Laughlin and offered to buy the property, which is now called the Riverside Resort. South Pointe was renamed Laughlin when the U.S. Postal Service inspector insisted Don Laughlin give the town a name in order to receive mail.

During the 1980s, a surge of casino construction exploded in Laughlin. The Colorado Hotel (now the Pioneer), the Regency, Sam's Town Gold River (now the River Palms) and the Edgewater opened early in the decade. The activity attracted other investors to begin a second boom resulting in the construction of the Colorado Belle that resembles a paddlewheel boat, Harrah's Del Rio, the railroad-theme Ramada Express with a miniature train running around the property. Finally, in 1990, the Flamingo Hilton was built followed in 1994 by Avi, an Indian casino.

Today there are nine hotel/casinos and one motel in Laughlin providing over 10,000 rooms, 125,000 square feet of meeting space, 60 restaurants, two museums, a 34-lane bowling center and a variety of boutiques, spas and salons and even an airport. This city by the river now attracts nearly five million visitors annually and hosts many high-profile special events.

### Jean, Goodsprings and Primm

Going less than an hour's drive west on I-15, you will encounter Primm located on the California border and a couple enticing stops along the way.

Halfway to Primm is a spot in the road called Jean, which you can't miss because of the two spectacular, turn-of-the-century theme hotels – the 812-room Gold Strike and 300-room Nevada Landing that looks like a landing with two paddlewheel boats pulled up to it.

If you turn off the road here and go 10 miles inland on state highway 53, you'll run into the ghost town of Goodsprings. The town was named after Mr. Joseph Good who headquartered his cattle-raising operation there. It was a mining camp with a hotel, a general store, and a saloon that is still operating.

The Pioneer Saloon was built in 1913 and it is America's only remaining all-tin structure made out of stamped metal.

*Callville Bay and Marina, Lake Mead*

*Opposite: Lee Canyon Ski Area*

The cherry wood bar was constructed in the 1880's in Brunswick, Maine. There are bullet holes through the walls and the pot-bellied stove still heats the saloon. Screen actress Carole Lombard died in a plane crash on the nearby Double Deal Mountain in 1942, and her husband, Clark Gable sat in the Pioneer Saloon for days after the tragedy. A small room at the side of the saloon offers artifacts and newspaper clippings.

Continuing on to Primm, formerly called State Line, you'll find a destination with three big casinos that suddenly pop up along I-15 and are connected by a tram system suspended over the interstate highway.

Whiskey Pete's is known as the "Castle in the Desert," and it has been rumored that Ol' Whiskey Pete himself is buried standing up out there and has watched over the property throughout the years. Two castle towers hold 777 rooms and suites.

Across the highway are the other two resorts. Buffalo Bill's Resort and Casino combines the Old West style with New West fun. It boasts two towers and 1,242 rooms, adventure rides, Star of the Desert Arena with major headliners and a giant buffalo-shaped swimming pool.

The third property is the 624-room Primm Valley Resort. It opened in May 1990 with a world's fair theme. The Fashion Outlet of Las Vegas with more than 100 designer outlets is connected to this property. Just four miles south of Primm at Valley Casino Resorts in California are two of the nation's top 100 public golf courses designed by Tom Fazio.

# The LVCVA and News Bureau

The Las Vegas Convention and Visitors Authority (LVCVA) is charged with marketing Southern Nevada as a tourism and convention destination worldwide, and also with operating the Las Vegas Convention Center and Cashman Center.

The original event-oriented Convention Center, which at the time had a modern-styled dome, was where the Beatles played during their famous Las Vegas visit in 1952 when they stayed at the Sahara Hotel.

Today with an expansive new convention center, approximately 133,000 hotel rooms in Las Vegas alone and nine million square feet of meeting and exhibit space citywide, the LVCVA's mission focuses on attracting ever-increasing numbers of leisure and business travelers to the area.

The Las Vegas Convention Center's first convention was held in April 1959 and drew 5,000 delegates. Almost three decades later, CONEXPO in 1987 drew 135,000 delegates.

On September 21, 1993, The Las Vegas Convention Center completed a $45 million renovation and expansion program. It had 1.8 million convention and meeting attendees in 1992. As of this date, Las Vegas services the largest tradeshows in the world and is unsurpassed as a convention site.

The Las Vegas News Bureau began in 1949 as the Desert Sea News Bureau, a publicity arm of the Las Vegas Chamber of Commerce. When the 1950s started there were four major resorts and by 1959, there were 15. This is the agency that on June 30, 1953, plugged publicist Al Freeman's best-remembered publicity hype, the Sands Floating Crap Game. The News Bureau photographers captured images of celebrities performing and playing in Las Vegas and sent them out via the newswire publications worldwide. Some images were serious like the atomic bomb testing; others farfetched, like taking a cheesecake photo and saying the gal was a fry cook. The credo for the hotel publicist at the time was "make sure you get the name of the hotel in the photograph."

Since 1992, the News Bureau has operated as part of the LVCVA's public relations department documenting Las Vegas' happenings and other Southern Nevada destinations. With such an awe-inspiring future, the Las Vegas News Bureau will always have something to write about…just like I do.

Is this the greatest job in the world, or what??? I live in the city I love, with the people I love, doing the thing I love! I hope you sensed my complete happiness in the work just completed. It has been a blast. Enjoy!

*Beautiful Mt. Charleston*

*Must see - Valley of Fire*

## ABOUT THE AUTHOR

Jackie Brett has written weekly about Las Vegas for more than 29 years while doing special stories for more than 20 different publications. She has been an integral part of the growth scene, keeping readers abreast of every happening from shows changing to new construction; special events to the huge shopping/dining explosion. During her first eight years, she interviewed over 250 headliners and casino figure heads while covering the lounge scene for *Panorama Magazine,* an insert in the former *Los Angeles Herald Examiner.*

Her Las Vegas and Laughlin syndicated columns appear in the *San Diego Union Tribune, Orange County Register, Ventura Star, Bakersfield Californian, Arizona Republic* and the *Las Vegas Leisure Guide,* as well as on her Web site, www.jackiebrett.com.

After a six-year Hollywood movie industry career, Jackie spent 16 years in the hotel/casino industry working for Circus Circus, the Silverbird, Sahara and Imperial Palace in marketing, entertainment and advertising.

For 13 years, she held numerous positions with *Nevada Magazine* and with the Nevada Commission on Tourism, ranging from group-travel marketing specialist to motorsports manager.

Needless to say, she is a gal well qualified to guide you on your book tour of Las Vegas. Join her for a fabulous visit!

# About the Photographer

Larry Hanna has been working as an advertising photographer in Las Vegas since 1976. He has done award-winning photography for most of the major resorts in Nevada. He frequently photographs in concert with his wife Peggy, who works internationally as a photostylist. He has earned Master of Photography and Craftsman Photographer degrees from the Professional Photographers of America. Larry is a four-time recipient of the prestigious Nevada Professional Photographer of the Year award.

Originally from the Washington, D.C. area, Larry pursued a career in medical research. After earning a Master of Science degree from Virginia Tech in biochemistry and completing his course work for his doctorate at Vanderbilt University, he followed his heart and moved to California to study photography. He has never looked back.

Larry tired of the crowded freeways of southern California and moved to Las Vegas where his parents had retired earlier. Las Vegas has grown from about 300,000 people when he arrived to approaching 2 million currently. He lives in the suburbs with his wife Peggy, two children, Brandon and Brittany (one in college and the other almost ready to go), and two dogs (Kodak and Rosie). He is an avid tennis player and enjoys traveling the Southwest. He'll be quick to tell you, "Life in Las Vegas is like anywhere else once you are off the Strip… "

With these credentials, he was a "shoe-in" first choice for our Las Vegas book.

*Teddy Bear Cholla and wildflowers remind us we are in the desert*

*Rear Cover: Desert cactus blossom*